MACHU PICCHU

Gillian Richardson
and Heather Kissock

www.av2books.com

MEDIA ENHANCED BOOKS
AV²
BY WEIGL™
ADDED VALUE • AUDIO VISUAL

AV² provides enriched content that supplements and complements this book Weigl's AV² books strive to create inspired learning and engage young minds in a total learning experience.

Your AV² Media Enhanced books come alive with...

Audio
Listen to sections of the book read aloud.

Key Words
Study vocabulary, and complete a matching word activity.

Go to **www.av2books.com**, and enter this book's unique code.

Video
Watch informative video clips.

Quizzes
Test your knowledge.

BOOK CODE

A397257

Embedded Weblinks
Gain additional information for research.

Slide Show
View images and captions, and prepare a presentation.

AV² by Weigl brings you media enhanced books that support active learning.

Try This!
Complete activities and hands-on experiments.

... and much, much more!

Published by AV² by Weigl
350 5th Avenue, 59th Floor
New York, NY 10118

Website: www.av2books.com   www.weigl.com

Library of Congress Cataloging-in-Publication Data
Richardson, Gillian.
 Machu Picchu / Gillian Richardson and Heather Kissock.
    p. cm. -- (Virtual field trip)
Includes index.
 ISBN 978-1-61913-250-4 (hardcover : alk. paper) --
 ISBN 978-1-61913-256-6 (softcover : alk. paper)
1. Machu Picchu Site (Peru)--Juvenile literature. 2. Inca architecture--Juvenile literature.
3. Peru--Antiquities--Juvenile literature. I. Kissock, Heather. II. Title.
 F3429.1.M3R533 2012
 985'.01--dc23

                    2011045490

Printed in the United States of America in North Mankato, Minnesota
1 2 3 4 5 6 7 8 9 0 16 15 14 13 12

012012
WEP060112

Editor: Heather Kissock
Design: Terry Paulhus

Every reasonable effort has been made to trace ownership and to obtain permission to reprint copyright material. The publishers would be pleased to have any errors or omissions brought to their attention so that they may be corrected in subsequent printings.

Weigl acknowledges Getty Images as its primary image supplier for this title.

Contents

What is Machu Picchu?

Some of the most exciting **archaeological** finds include the remains of human structures built long ago. In remote places, such as forests, the discovery of these remains is often unexpected. They lead to new knowledge about the ancient cultures and civilizations that built them. Machu Picchu is such a place.

Machu Picchu is often called the "Lost City of the Inca." The Inca were a tribe that lived in Peru in the 13th century. Hidden by thick forest plants high in the Andes Mountains of South America, the Inca city lay abandoned for nearly 400 years. It was not until 1911 that the area became active again. At this time, Hiram Bingham, an assistant professor from Yale University, came upon the city's ruins.

When the overgrown forest was cut back, a community of 150 to 200 buildings was revealed. It included sacred temples and an **irrigated** farming area for growing crops. At its peak, about 1,000 people likely lived and worked in the city.

Machu Picchu means "old peak" in Quechua, the language spoken by the Incas.

Snapshot of Peru

Peru is located in western South America. The Pacific Ocean serves as its western border. Chile and Bolivia lie to Peru's south, while Brazil shares its eastern border. Ecuador and Colombia are located north of Peru.

INTRODUCING PERU

CAPITAL CITY: Lima

FLAG:

POPULATION: 29,248,943 (2011)

OFFICIAL LANGUAGES: Spanish and Quechua

CURRENCY: Nuevo Sol

CLIMATE: Tropical climate in the east, desert climate in the west, frigid at high altitudes

SUMMER TEMPERATURE: 77° to 83° Fahrenheit (25° to 28° Celsius)

WINTER TEMPERATURE: 54° to 59° F (12° to 15° C)

TIME ZONE: Peru Time (PET)

COLOMBIA

ECUADOR

P E R U

BRAZIL

ANDES MOUNTAINS

Lima

Lake Titicaca

BOLIVIA

Pacific Ocean

Peru

--·--· International Boundary

★ National Capital

∧ Mountains

| 0 | 500 miles |
| 0 | 500 kilometers |

N

Spanish Words to Know

When visiting a foreign country, it is always a good idea to know some words and phrases of the local language. Practice the phrases below to prepare for a trip to Peru.

Perdone
Excuse me/Sorry

Hola!
Hello

gracias
Thank you

Habla ingles?
Do you speak English?

Si
Yes

Cuanto cuesta?
How much is it?

Me llamo...
My name is

adios
Goodbye

Me puedes ayudar?
Can you help me?

No
No

Como esta?
How are you?

Como se llama?
What is your name?

A Step Back in Time

Machu Picchu was built on the orders of Pachacuti. He was the ruler of the Incas from 1438 to 1471. Some historians believe that he ordered the construction of Machu Picchu to celebrate the defeat of the Inca's enemies, the Chancas.

Machu Picchu is believed to have been built from 1460 to 1470. When Pachacuti first started building it, Machu Picchu was meant to be part royal estate and part religious **retreat**. It would house the emperor, as well as his family, spiritual and political advisors, and servants.

CONSTRUCTION TIMELINE

AD 1438 to 1471
Pachacuti becomes emperor. He begins constructing buildings and roads throughout the land.

1460 to 1470
Pachacuti builds Machu Picchu.

Early 1500s
Machu Picchu is abandoned when the Spanish invade the area.

1911
American professor Hiram Bingham finds the ruins of Machu Picchu.

Francisco Pizarro was a conquistador from Spain. He played a key role in bringing down the Inca empire in the 1530s. He was responsible for dethroning and killing the Inca emperor at that time, Atahualpa.

Hiram Bingham had been searching for a city called Vilcabamba when a local farmer led him to the ruins of Machu Picchu. Bingham later found Vilcabamba deep in the forest west of Cuzco.

Machu Picchu was one of the many construction projects built during Pachacuti's reign. The ruins of this city are an example of the architectural and engineering skills of the ancient Inca people. Besides houses, the Inca built temples for worship and used a natural spring that was thought to be sacred as a source of clean water. A gravity-fed system ran through stone channels to irrigate the crops that were farmed on the **terraced** fields.

Pachacuti was Peru's ninth emperor.

1950 to 1980
Major restoration efforts take place. By 1980, about one third of the site has been restored.

1981
Peru declares Machu Picchu and its surrounding areas a historical **sanctuary**.

1983
Machu Picchu is designated a **UNESCO World Heritage Site**.

2007
Machu Picchu is named one of the **New Seven Wonders of the World**.

Restoration efforts included engineers and local laborers. During the restoration, workers numbered the rocks according to their location on the site.

Machu Picchu's Location

Machu Picchu is located about 70 miles (113 km) from Cuzco, the capital city of the ancient Inca Empire. Machu Picchu's ruins are found at the top of a ridge between two mountain peaks, invisible from the forest and winding Urubamba River gorge below.

Machu Picchu sits on the Inca Trail. The Inca Trail is part of a 14,291-mile (23,000-km) system of trails that covers much of South America. The trails were initially built for military purposes. However, the best-known part of the trail—the route to Machu Picchu—was a royal road. It was used only for religious and ceremonial purposes.

Huayna Picchu is the peak closest to Machu Picchu. To the Inca, Machu Pichu's royal estate symbolized the emperor's face. Huayna Picchu was the emperor's nose. As the mountain points to the sky, the Inca believed that the emperor was looking towards the gods.

Machu Picchu Today

For almost four centuries after it was abandoned by the Inca, nature took over Machu Picchu, all but hiding it from human view. The walls, stairways, and buildings lay beneath thick forest vines, underbrush, and moss. They were protected from the rainforest climate. Shrouded in fog and drenched in heavy rain, the stonework of the city remained intact. Since its discovery in 1911, restoration efforts have been ongoing. Today, Machu Picchu is a well-known tourist site. In one year, the ruins can host up to 400,000 people from around the world.

Elevation The ancient city was built 7,710 feet (2,350 m) above sea level.

Stairs In all, about 100 stairways, containing 3,000 individual stairs, connect parts of Machu Picchu.

Area The buildings and terraced farmland of Machu Picchu cover an area of 5 square miles (13 sq. km).

5 square miles (13 sq. km)

The Agricultural Sector

Machu Picchu is divided into the agricultural sector and the urban sector. The agricultural sector is located on the southern end of the site. Here, crops were grown to feed the people living at Machu Picchu.

Terraces Crops could not grow on the steep slopes of the mountains. For this reason, the Inca built level terraces, or steps, into the mountainside. Machu Picchu has 120 terraces of varying heights. Some can be up to 13 feet (4 m) high. Only the upper terraces were used for farming. The lower terraces were used to keep the upper levels stable and control **erosion**. The terraces have their own **aqueducts.** These provided water for irrigating crops.

There are two layers of terraces. They are divided by a path that appears to be part of the Inca Trail.

The Funerary Rock is made of granite. It has three steps carved into its side and a ring that points to the sky. No one knows the meaning of these carvings.

Cemetery A grouping of tombs lies along the west side of the agricultural sector. Within the cemetery is a large stone known as the Funerary Rock. It is believed that this rock may have been used to prepare the dead for burial or for religious **rituals.**

The House of the Guardians sits on one of the highest points in Machu Picchu. This position allowed the guards to see miles (km) beyond the city.

House of the Guardians The House of the Guardians sits at the top of the agricultural sector. It provides a view of both the agricultural and urban sectors of Machu Picchu. The building has three walls and several windows.

The Sun Gate looks down on Machu Picchu, affording visitors a complete view of the site.

Sun Gate The Sun Gate is an entrance to Machu Picchu that can only be accessed by hiking into the site on the Inca Trail. The gate features a series of stone buildings linked by corridors and steep stone stairways.

City Gate The city gate is a large doorway through which people left the agricultural sector and entered the urban sector. It was the only way to enter the city from the southeast and was used primarily by residents of Machu Picchu. The city gate was well protected and featured a sturdy system of locks.

At one time, the city gate had a large, wooden door.

Qolqas The qolqas are a series of small stone huts located on the terraces. These huts were used for storage. It is believed that grains and other crops were kept here until needed.

Qolqas are found on Machu Picchu's terraces and inside the city itself. They are also situated at specific intervals along the Inca Trail.

VIRTUAL TOUR

It has been discovered that 60 percent of the Machu Picchu ruins are below ground level.

The Urban Sector

The urban sector contained the main buildings of Machu Picchu. This sector itself was divided into three districts. The Sacred District was used for religious purposes, while the Popular District contained houses and workshops. The Royal District housed the emperor and other nobility.

Temple of the Sun Machu Picchu's buildings include religious shrines, temples, and a royal tomb. The round Temple of the Sun is believed to have been used as a solar **observatory**. It houses a window through which light from the rising Sun enters on the June 21 **solstice**.

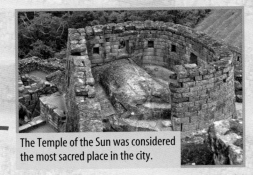

The Temple of the Sun was considered the most sacred place in the city.

Intihuatana Stone This sacred structure was used as a calendar. The 6-foot (1.8-m), 4-sided tower acted as a **sundial** to determine midday on the exact date of the spring and fall **equinox**. On March 21 and September 21, the Sun is directly over the tower, so it casts no shadow. The Inca believed they could capture the power of the Sun at this special time.

The Intihuatana Stone has been carved from a single piece of rock.

Popular District This part of the urban sector was where workers and their families lived. It is made up mainly of houses and qolqas. The rooms in these houses are much smaller than those found in the royal houses.

The Popular District also housed Machu Picchu's military staff.

Visitors are not allowed inside the Royal Tomb.

Royal Tomb A stairway near the Temple of the Sun leads down to the Royal Tomb. The entrance to the tomb features a rock carved into three stairs. The interior of the tomb is actually a natural cave. Several **niches** have been built into its walls.

Royal Group The Royal Group is a cluster of buildings that are thought to have housed the king and important officials. This belief is based on the large rooms inside as well as the location of the entrance and exit. Both are in the same place. This is believed to have helped maintain the security of the building.

The houses in the Royal Group are arranged in rows along a slope.

Big Ideas Behind Machu Picchu

Builders must plan how a structure will look before workers can begin the construction process. The people who built Machu Picchu adapted the forms of their structures to the conditions of the landscape as much as possible. Using their knowledge of scientific principles, the Inca created buildings and other structures that were both useful and pleasing to look at.

The terraced fields built on the steep hillsides are still level enough to be farmed today.

Understanding Weight

Machu Picchu was built from a type of stone called granite. Granite is very heavy. Such a heavy material needs a solid foundation beneath it for stable construction. The site at the top of the ridge where Machu Picchu is now located had to be leveled and prepared. The Inca used gravel and stone to support the weight of the walls, buildings, and terraces. This careful engineering has prevented the city from shifting due to heavy rain or the weight of so many huge stones. Even today, Machu Picchu's granite walls remain largely intact.

Geometry and Angles

The rocks used to build Machu Picchu came in different shapes and sizes. It was the job of the builders to shape the rocks so that they would fit together. Instead of creating blocks, the builders refined the original shape of the rock by cutting and smoothing it into straight lines. They then worked to match rocks that fit together. Finding rocks that fight tightly together was key to the structure's success. To make a strong structure, the rocks had to be matched up so that no spaces were left between them. The Inca did not use any form of **mortar** or cement to hold the rocks in place. The goal was to have the differently shaped rocks link like a jigsaw puzzle so that they would stay together.

Many of the doors and windows found in Machu Picchu have a trapezoid shape. Trapezoids are four-sided figures that have two parallel and two non-parallel sides.

Science at Work at Machu Picchu

Machu Picchu's impressive stone structures were built by hand. The Inca understood the science of their natural world and of construction. They used this knowledge, as well as physical labor, to cut, shape, and move the heavy stones.

The granite rocks were different sizes and shapes, some with as many as 32 corners.

Moving the Rock

Although the granite was located at the building site, its heavy weight would have made it difficult to move into place. The process of construction at Machu Picchu is not known, but it is possible that Inca workers used a method similar to other projects of the time. Near Lake Titicaca, south of Cuzco, stones for another city's construction were dragged by laborers, using ropes made of vines and hemp. Given the size of some granite blocks at Machu Picchu, it would have taken many laborers and a great deal of time to move them even a short distance. This may be why it took 10 years to build the city.

Cutting the Rock

Machu Picchu was constructed of white granite taken from an on-site **quarry**. Without the aid of power tools to cut the stones from the quarry, Inca workers relied on the natural features of the rock to help them instead. They may have used the principle of the wedge to split larger pieces into those of a more manageable size. A wedge is a simple pointed tool used to separate two objects when force is applied. Such a tool might have been made from bronze, the hardest metal that was available to the Inca. The wedge would have been hammered into cracks in the rock, forcing it to break apart.

A chisel is a type of wedge that can be used, along with a mallet, to shape rock.

VIRTUAL TOUR

Some of the blocks of granite used to construct Machu Picchu weigh more than 50 tons (45 tonnes).

Machu Picchu's Builders

While Pachacuti was responsible for the building of Machu Picchu, the hard labor was done by others. Stonemasons, stone carvers, metalworks, laborers, roof thatchers, and farmers were among the people who worked on the construction of the site.

Besides the Inca Trail, people can also hike up Huayna Picchu. The climb is steep, but once at the top, there are more buildings and ruins to explore.

Pachacuti Inca Ruler

Inca society consisted of a ruler who was part of a royal family, nobles and priests, and common people. Their influence remained limited until around AD 1438, when another group of people from the north attacked Cuzco. The Inca king, Wiracocha, fled, leaving his son Yupanqui to fight the enemy. Yupanqui won this battle. He changed his name to Pachacuti, which means "the one who rules everything," and began to extend his control within the country now known as Peru.

From 1438 to 1471, Inca power continued to grow. By the late 1400s, Pachacuti ruled an empire of about 10 million people that stretched from present-day Ecuador to Chile. As the Inca Empire grew, skilled engineers and architects built as many as 14,000 miles (22,531 km) of stone roads, known as the Inca Trail. Hundreds of white granite buildings were also built. Machu Picchu was likely built during this time.

No single architect or construction engineer is known to have built Machu Picchu. However, Pachacuti likely consulted with priests and astronomers to plan the orientation of the city.

Pachacuti died in 1471 after more than 30 years as the Inca ruler. He was succeeded by his son, Topa.

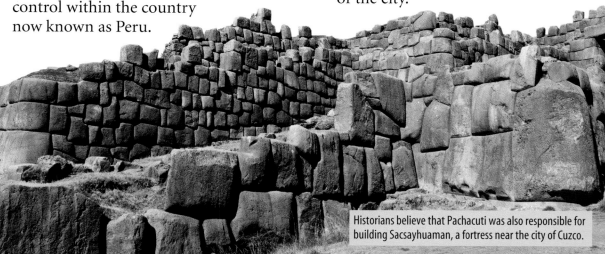

Historians believe that Pachacuti was also responsible for building Sacsayhuaman, a fortress near the city of Cuzco.

Stonemasons

The Inca used of a method of **dry stone construction** to build walls, structures, steps, and terraces. As part of this process, stonemasons took blocks of granite from a quarry within Machu Picchu. The blocks were then cut using stone and bronze tools. They were polished using sand or other stones to create flat surfaces. The finished blocks, called ashlar, were fitted together so tightly that they did not need mortar to hold them in place. This method creates a wall stable enough to withstand earthquake motion.

The craft of stonemasonry is still used worldwide to create buildings, structures, and sculptures.

Laborers

Laborers were responsible for doing many tasks during the construction of Machu Picchu. They helped to level the ground before buildings were constructed. They also moved granite blocks from the quarry to each building site and helped to lift them into place. Some laborers constructed the stepped terraces where the city's food supply was grown. Others built the water irrigation system.

Laborers today continue to play a role in the building of roads and pathways.

Roof Thatchers

Thatched roofs are not as common as they used to be. However, they are seeing a rebirth due to the trend toward using natural building materials.

Most of the buildings at Machu Picchu had **thatched** roofs. Making a thatched roof requires skilled workers. They must understand the materials and processes involved in using plants to make a roof that does not leak. To make the roofs at Machu Picchu, the thatchers chose a coarse grass called *ichu*. The thatchers would tie the *ichu* into bundles and fasten them to the roof beams. They placed many layers of bundles down the roof. The end thatches were tied to pegs that stuck out from the roof. This kept them from being blown away. When done properly, the roof would protect the inside of the building for 10 to 15 years. At that time, the thatching would be redone.

Similar Structures Around the World

The Inca were just one group of people to realize the durability of stone. People from different parts of the world have been using stone to construct buildings for thousands of years. Many of these structures still exist today—some in their entirety and others in part. The lasting quality of stone construction has ensured that something of these ancient structures remain for people today to learn about life in the past.

Great Pyramid

BUILT: 2600–2480 BC
LOCATION: Giza, Egypt
DESIGN: King Khufu
DESCRIPTION: The Great Pyramid is one of the three pyramids at Giza. This structure was built of cut stone blocks. The pyramid is thought to have about 2,300,000 blocks in total, more than any other structure ever built.

Some of the temples at Tikal are more than 200 feet (61 m) high.

The stones in the Great Pyramid weigh between 2.5 and 15 tons (2.2 and 13.6 tonnes).

Tikal

BUILT: 800–200 BC
LOCATION: Guatemala
DESIGN: Yax Ehb' Xook
DESCRIPTION: Tikal was a major site of **Mayan** civilization. This site is built of cut stone and has thousands of structures, including five temples and several public plazas that are accessed by ramps. Much of the site is still buried by mounds of earth and forest plants. It was occupied from the 6th century BC to the 10th century AD.

Angkor Wat

BUILT: 1140 AD
LOCATION: Angkor, Cambodia
DESIGN: King Suryavarman II
DESCRIPTION: This Hindu temple, built of stone masonry, was originally enclosed by a moat and wall. A 213-foot (65-m) tower in the center was built without mortar, similar to walls in Machu Picchu. Abandoned in 1431, Angkor Wat is one of the world's largest religious structures.

The towers of Angkor Wat have been designed to look like lotus buds.

Mont St. Michel is located on the border between the French provinces of Normandy and Brittany.

Mont St. Michel

BUILT: 1203 and later
LOCATION: Mont St. Michel, France
DESIGN: William de Volpiano
DESCRIPTION: This monastery built of cut stone sits on an island in Normandy. It was once connected to mainland France by a land bridge that was submerged at high tide. The bridge later became a **causeway**. Mont St. Michel was named by UNESCO as a World Heritage Site in 1979.

Issues Facing Machu Picchu

Thousands of people visit Machu Picchu every year. This number of people can have a major impact on the site and its surroundings. The Peruvian government is taking several steps that help to protect the site as well as allow tourists to continue their visits.

WHAT IS THE ISSUE?

The stonework is being harmed by the large number of people who explore the site.	Many people do not take their trash with them when they leave the site.	People can travel to Machu Picchu in a variety of ways, from bus to train. Some people hike into the site on their own.

EFFECTS

Touching and walking on the ruins are causing them to erode.	Pollution is damaging the fragile **ecosystem** in and around Machu Picchu.	It is difficult to control the number of people visiting the site.

ACTION TAKEN

After being declared a UNESCO World Heritage Site in 1983, the site receives support from the United Nations in its conservation efforts.	In 2003, a waste removal system was implemented that sees garbage collected and taken to disposal sites in nearby communities.	The government has capped the daily number of visitors to the site at 2,500. Hikers must be part of an official tour. Tourists can stay at the site for only four days.

Make a Star Clock

The Inca used the Sun, Moon, and stars as a calendar. Try making this star clock to help you find out the date and time.

Materials
- paper
- pencil
- bristleboard or other cardboard
- wristwatch

Instructions

1. On a piece of paper, draw two circles like the ones on this page. Copy the pictures and words onto the two circles, and cut the circles from the paper.

2. Place the small circle on top of the large circle. Push a pencil through the center of both circles to hold them together.

3. On a clear night, go outside. Find the North Star, as shown on the face of your star clock. Face the North Star.

4. Find the current month around the outside circle of the star clock. Put your thumb over the current month. Hold the star clock so your thumb is at the top.

5. Turn the smaller circle until its stars look the same as those in the sky.

6. Read the time in the window. If you are on Daylight Savings Time, add one hour. How does the star clock's time compare to the time on the wristwatch?

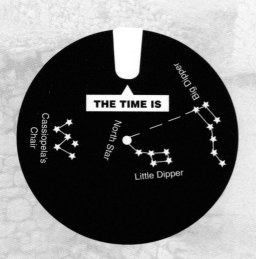

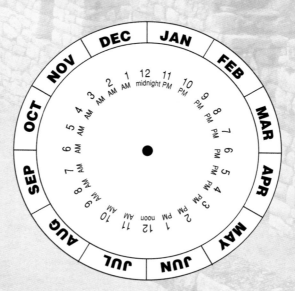

Machu Picchu Quiz

Q Why was Machu Picchu so hard to find?

A It was hidden on a mountaintop ridge deep in the forest and was covered in vegetation.

Q What special construction style did the ancient Inca use to build walls in Machu Picchu?

A They used dry stone construction with granite blocks.

Q Why did the Inca build terraced agricultural fields?

A It was not possible to grow crops on the steep slopes of mountains in Peru.

Q What is the Intihuatana Stone?

A It is a pillar of rock that acts like a sundial to show the spring and fall equinox.

Words to Know

aqueducts: channels designed to transport water from a remote source

archaeological: studying the past by digging up and examining old structures and objects

causeway: a raised path or road that crosses water

dry stone construction: made without mortar

ecosystem: a community of living things

equinox: the time of year when there are equal hours of daylight and darkness

erosion: the wearing away of rock by ice, wind, or rain

irrigated: supplied with water

Mayan: an American Indian of Mexico and Central America

mortar: a building material like cement that hardens to hold objects together

New Seven Wonders of the World: seven structures considered by scholars to be the most wondrous of the world

niches: recesses in a wall

observatory: a building used to study the sky

quarry: a pit from which stone is obtained

retreat: a place for religious study

rituals: ceremonies used in a place of worship

sanctuary: a sacred place

solstice: the time when the Sun is farthest from the equator

sundial: a device that measures time by showing the position of the Sun

terraced: set on a series of level platforms that are built on a steep slope to create farmland on otherwise unusable terrain

thatched: covered with a natural vegetation

UNESCO World Heritage Site: a site designated by the United Nations to be of great cultural worth to the world and in need of protection

Index

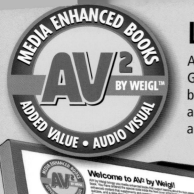

Log on to www.av2books.com

AV² by Weigl brings you media enhanced books that support active learning. Go to www.av2books.com, and enter the special code found on page 2 of this book. You will gain access to enriched and enhanced content that supplements and complements this book. Content includes video, audio, weblinks, quizzes, a slide show, and activities.

Audio
Listen to sections of the book read aloud.

Video
Watch informative video clips.

Embedded Weblinks
Gain additional information for research.

Try This!
Complete activities and hands-on experiments.

WHAT'S ONLINE?

Try This!	Embedded Weblinks	Video	EXTRA FEATURES
Identify the features of Machu Picchu.	Learn more about Machu Picchu and its relationship with UNESCO.	Tour Machu Picchu by watching a video.	
Imagine that you are designing Machu Picchu.	Learn more about the theories surrounding the creation of Machu Picchu.	See the Sun rise over Machu Picchu.	
Test your knowledge of Machu Picchu.	Find out who the Inca were.		

Audio
Listen to sections of the book read aloud.

Key Words
Study vocabulary, and complete a matching word activity.

Slide Show
View images and caption and prepare a presentati

Quizzes
Test your knowledge.

AV² was built to bridge the gap between print and digital. We encourage you to tell us what you like and what you want to see in the future.

Sign up to be an AV² Ambassador at www.av2books.com/ambassador.